THIS WALKER BOOK BELONGS TO:

_____

_____

_____

_____

For Minky

The publisher gratefully acknowledges permission to use the following material:

"Cats" from *The Children's Bells* by Eleanor Farjeon, published by Oxford University Press.
Reprinted by permission of David Higham Associates.

"Ducks' Ditty" from *The Wind in the Willows* by Kenneth Grahame, © The University Chest, Oxford.
Reproduced by permission of Curtis Brown, London.

"Eletelephony" from *Tirra Lirra* by Laura E Richards. Copyright © 1963 by Laura E Richards;
copyright © renewed. Reprinted by permission of Little, Brown and Company.

"Kitchen Sink-Song" by Tony Mitton, © Tony Mitton.
Reprinted by permission of David Higham Associates Limited.

"Merry Christmas" from *Feathered Ones and Furry* by Aileen Fisher.
Copyright © 1971 Aileen Fisher. Reprinted by permission of Marian Reiner for the author.

"Mice" from *Fifty-one New Nursery Rhymes* by Rose Fyleman.
Reprinted by permission of The Society of Authors as the
Literary Representative of the Estate of Rose Fyleman.

"The More It Snows" from *The House at Pooh Corner* by A A Milne,
published by Methuen Children's Books 11.10.28. Reprinted by permission of Reed Consumer Books.

"On the Ning Nang Nong" © Spike Milligan Productions Ltd, from *Silly Verse for Kids*, published by Puffin Books.

"Oodles of Noodles" by Lucia and James Hymes, Jr, © 1964 Lucia and James Hymes, Jr.
Reprinted by permission of Addison Wesley Longman.

"The Tickle Rhyme" from *The Monster Horse* by Ian Serraillier,
published by Oxford University Press. Reprinted by permission of Anne Serraillier.

"Who Likes Cuddles?" from *Don't Put Mustard in the Custard* by Michael Rosen
© Michael Rosen, 1985. First published by André Deutsch Children's Books,
an imprint of Scholastic Ltd.

While every effort has been made to obtain permission,
there may still be cases in which we have failed to
trace a copyright holder, and we would like to
apologize for any apparent negligence.

First published 1999 by Walker Books Ltd
87 Vauxhall Walk, London SE11 5HJ

This edition published 2002

2 4 6 8 10 9 7 5 3

This selection © 1999 Walker Books
Illustrations © 1999 Harry Horse

This book has been typeset in Goudy

Printed in Hong Kong

British Library Cataloguing in Publication Data:
a catalogue record for this book is
available from the British Library

ISBN 0-7445-8919-3

Higglety Pigglety POP!

and Other First Poems

illustrated by

Harry Horse

WALKER BOOKS
AND SUBSIDIARIES
LONDON · BOSTON · SYDNEY

Contents

The Owl and the Pussy-cat
page 6

Fried Fresh Fish
page 8

Peas
page 8

Fuzzy Wuzzy
page 9

The Man Who Wasn't There
page 9

On the Ning Nang Nong
page 10

There Was an Old Man with a Beard
page 11

Cats
page 12

The More It Snows
page 14

Merry Christmas
page 15

Turtle Soup
page 16

Oodles of Noodles
page 17

I Love You
page 18

Question
page 18

Valentine
page 19

Ducks' Ditty
page 20

If All the World Were Paper
page 22

The Purple Cow
page 23

A Wise Old Owl
page 24

Higglety, Pigglety, Pop!
page 24

Clocks
page 25

Kitchen Sink-Song
page 25

Eletelephony
page 26

Mice
page 28

The Tickle Rhyme
page 29

Who Likes Cuddles?
page 30

The Owl and the Pussy-cat

The Owl and the Pussy-cat went to sea
In a beautiful pea-green boat,
They took some honey, and plenty of money,
Wrapped up in a five-pound note.
The Owl looked up to the stars above,
And sang to a small guitar,
"O lovely Pussy! O Pussy, my love,
What a beautiful Pussy you are,
You are,
You are!
What a beautiful Pussy you are!"

Pussy said to the Owl, "You elegant fowl!
How charmingly sweet you sing!
O let us be married! too long we have tarried:
But what shall we do for a ring?"
They sailed away, for a year and a day,
To the land where the Bong-tree grows
And there in a wood a Piggy-wig stood
With a ring at the end of his nose,
His nose,
His nose,
With a ring at the end of his nose.

"Dear Pig, are you willing to sell for one shilling
Your ring?" Said the Piggy, "I will."
So they took it away, and were married next day
By the Turkey who lives on the hill.
They dined on mince, and slices of quince,
Which they ate with a runcible spoon;
And hand in hand, on the edge of the sand,
They danced by the light of the moon,
The moon,
The moon,
They danced by the light of the moon.

Edward Lear

Fried Fresh Fish

Fried fresh fish,
Fish fried fresh,
Fresh fried fish,
Fresh fish fried,
Or fish fresh fried.

Anon

Peas

I eat my peas with honey,
I've done it all my life,
It makes them taste quite funny,
But it keeps them on the knife.

Anon

Fuzzy Wuzzy

Fuzzy Wuzzy was a bear;
Fuzzy Wuzzy had no hair.
So Fuzzy Wuzzy wasn't fuzzy. Was he?

Anon

The Man Who Wasn't There

As I was going up the stair
I met a man who wasn't there.
He wasn't there again today –
Oh, how I wish he'd go away.

Anon

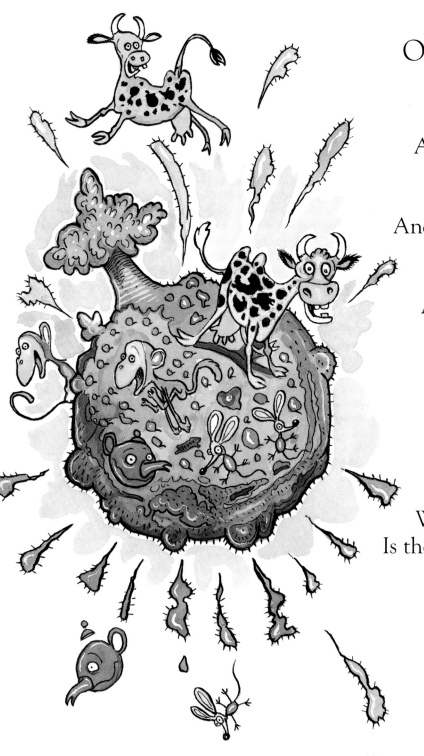

On the Ning Nang Nong

On the Ning Nang Nong
Where the Cows go Bong!
And the Monkeys all say Boo!
There's a Nong Nang Ning
Where the trees go Ping!
And the tea pots Jibber Jabber Joo.
On the Nong Ning Nang
All the mice go Clang!
And you just can't catch 'em
when they do!
So it's Ning Nang Nong!
Cows go Bong!
Nong Nang Ning!
Trees go Ping!
Nong Ning Nang!
The mice go Clang!
What a noisy place to belong,
Is the Ning Nang Ning Nang Nong!!

Spike Milligan

There Was an Old Man with a Beard

There was an Old Man with a beard,
Who said, "It is just as I feared! –
Two Owls and a Hen, four Larks and a Wren,
Have all built their nests in my beard!"

Edward Lear

Cats

Cats sleep
Anywhere,
Any table,
Any chair,
Top of piano,
Window-ledge,
In the middle,
On the edge,
Open drawer,
Empty shoe,
Anybody's
Lap will do,

Fitted in a
Cardboard box,
In the cupboard
With your frocks –
Anywhere!
They don't care!
Cats sleep
Anywhere.

Eleanor Farjeon

The More It Snows

The more it
SNOWS-tiddely-pom,
The more it
GOES-tiddely-pom
The more it
GOES-tiddely-pom
On
Snowing.

And nobody
KNOWS-tiddely-pom,
How cold my
TOES-tiddely-pom
How cold my
TOES-tiddely-pom
Are
Growing.

A A Milne

Merry Christmas

I saw on the snow
when I tried my skis
the track of a mouse
beside some trees.

Before he tunneled
to reach his house
he wrote "Merry Christmas"
in white, in mouse.

Aileen Fisher

15

Turtle Soup

Beautiful Soup, so rich and green,
Waiting in a hot tureen!
Who for such dainties would not stoop?
Soup of the evening, beautiful Soup!
Soup of the evening, beautiful Soup!
Beau–ootiful Soo–oop!
Beau–ootiful Soo–oop!
Soo–oop of the e–e–evening,
Beautiful, beautiful Soup!

Beautiful Soup! Who cares for fish,
Game, or any other dish?
Who would not give all else for two
pennyworth only of beautiful Soup?
Pennyworth only of beautiful Soup?
Beau–ootiful Soo–oop!
Beau–ootiful Soo–oop!
Soo–oop of the e–e–evening,
Beautiful, beauti–FUL SOUP!

Lewis Carroll

Oodles of Noodles

I love noodles. Give me oodles.
Make a mound up to the sun.
Noodles are my favourite foodles.
I eat noodles by the ton.

Lucia and James L Hymes, Jr

I Love You

I love you, I love you,
I love you divine,
Please give me your bubble gum,
You're *sitting* on mine!

Anon

Question

Do you love me
Or do you not?
You told me once
But I forgot.

Anon

Valentine

I got a valentine from

Timmy
Jimmy
Tillie
Billie
Nicky
Micky
Ricky
Dicky
Laura
Nora
Cora
Flora
Donnie
Ronnie
Lonnie
Connie

Eva even sent me two
But I didn't get *none* from you.

Shel Silverstein

Ducks' Ditty

All along the backwater,
Through the rushes tall,
Ducks are a-dabbling.
Up tails all!

Ducks' tails, drakes' tails,
Yellow feet a-quiver,
Yellow bills all out of sight
Busy in the river!

Slushy green undergrowth
Where the roach swim –
Here we keep our larder,
Cool and full and dim.

Every one for what he likes!
We like to be
Heads down, tails up,
Dabbling free!

High in the blue above
Swifts whirl and call –
We are down a-dabbling
Up tails all!

Kenneth Grahame

If All the World Were Paper

If all the world were paper,
And all the sea were ink;
And all the trees were bread and cheese,
What should we do for drink?

Anon

The Purple Cow

I never saw a Purple Cow,
I never hope to see one;
But I can tell you, anyhow,
I'd rather see than be one.

Gelett Burgess

A Wise Old Owl

A wise old owl sat in an oak,
The more he heard, the less he spoke;
The less he spoke, the more he heard.
Why aren't we all like that wise old bird?

Anon

Higglety, Pigglety, Pop!

Higglety, pigglety, pop!
The dog has eaten the mop;
The pig's in a hurry,
The cat's in a flurry,
Higglety, pigglety, pop!

Samuel Goodrich

Clocks

What does the clock in the hall say?
Tick, tock, tick, tock.
What does the clock in the room say?
Tick, tick, tick, tick, tick, tick, tick, tick.
What do little watches all say?
Tick-a, tick-a, tick-a, tick-a, tick-a, tick-a, tick.

Anon

Kitchen Sink-Song

Tap goes drip-drip
plip-plip-plink.
Tap goes trickle at the
kitchen sink.
Fridge goes gurgle
Pan goes slop.
Bin goes flip-flap
Toast goes POP!

Tony Mitton

Eletelephony

Once there was an elephant,
Who tried to use the telephant –
No! no! I mean an elephone
Who tried to use the telephone –
(Dear me! I am not certain quite
That even now I've got it right.)

Howe'er it was, he got his trunk
Entangled in the telephunk;
The more he tried to get it free,
The louder buzzed the telephee –
(I fear I'd better drop the song
Of elephop and telephong!)

Laura E Richards

Mice

I think mice
Are rather nice.

Their tails are long,
Their faces small,
They haven't any
Chins at all.
Their ears are pink,
Their teeth are white,
They run about
The house at night.
They nibble things
They shouldn't touch
And no one seems
To like them much.

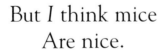

But *I* think mice
Are nice.

Rose Fyleman

The Tickle Rhyme

"Who's that tickling my back?" said the wall.
"Me," said a small
caterpillar. "I'm learning
to crawl."

Ian Serraillier

Who Likes Cuddles?

Who likes cuddles?
Me.
Who likes hugs?
Me.

Who likes tickles?
Me.
Who likes getting their face stroked?
Me.
Who likes being lifted up high?
Me.

Who likes sitting on laps?
Me.
Who likes being whirled round and round?
Me.

But best of all I like
getting into bed and getting blowy blowy
down my neck behind my ear.
A big warm tickly blow
lovely.

Michael Rosen